If I Were a Shark

By Meg Gaertner

level 2 little blue readers

www.littlebluehousebooks.com

Little Blue House is distributed by North Star Editions:
sales@northstareditions.com | 888-417-0195

Produced for Little Blue House by Red Line Editorial.

Photographs ©: Shutterstock Images, cover, 18 (bottom), 24 (bottom left); iStockphoto, 4, 7, 8–9, 10, 12–13, 14–15, 16–17, 18 (top), 21, 23, 24 (top left), 24 (top right), 24 (bottom right)

Library of Congress Control Number: 2020913851

ISBN
978-1-64619-306-6 (hardcover)
978-1-64619-324-0 (paperback)
978-1-64619-360-8 (ebook pdf)
978-1-64619-342-4 (hosted ebook)

Printed in the United States of America
Mankato, MN
012021

About the Author

Meg Gaertner enjoys reading, writing, dancing, and being outside. She thinks sharks are fascinating, even though they scare her a bit. She lives in Minnesota.

Table of Contents

ocean

If I Were a Shark

I would swim

in the ocean.

I would move my strong tail.

I would zip through
the water.

skin

Body Parts

I would have bumpy skin.

It would help me

move fast.

I would have good eyes. They would help me see in dark water.

I would have sharp teeth.
They would help me
eat food.

teeth

I would have gills
on my sides.
These openings would
help me breathe.

Finding Food

I would look for seals.

I would jump out
of the water.

I would catch my food.

Glossary

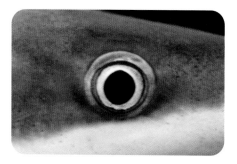

eye

tail

seal

teeth

Index